December 2001

NORTH AMERICAN FREE TRADE AGREEMENT

Coordinated Operational Plan Needed to Ensure Mexican Trucks' Compliance With U.S. Standards

G A O
Accountability ★ Integrity ★ Reliability

GAO-02-238

Contents

Letter		1
	Results in Brief	2
	Background	3
	Relatively Few Mexican Carriers Initially Expected Beyond Border Commercial Zones	7
	The United States and Most U.S. Border States Are Not Prepared to Ensure That Mexican Commercial Carriers Meet U.S. Safety Standards	12
	Mexico Has Taken Steps to Improve Commercial Vehicle Safety and Emissions, But Extent of Compliance With U.S. Standards Remains Unclear	20
	Conclusions	27
	Recommendation for Executive Action	28
	Agency Comments and Our Evaluation	28
Appendix I	**Scope and Methodology**	31
Appendix II	**Space Available for Truck Inspections at Southwest Border Ports of Entry**	33
Appendix III	**Comments From the U.S. Customs Service**	35
Appendix IV	**GAO Contacts and Staff Acknowledgments**	36
	GAO Contact	36
	Acknowledgments	36
Tables		
	Table 1: Truck Crossings From Mexico into the United States, Fiscal Year 2001	5
	Table 2: Registration Fees for International Registration Plan Members and Non-members	9
	Table 3: Space Designated for Truck Inspection Activities at Southwest Border Commercial Ports of Entry, as of November 2001	33

Figures

Figure 1: Commercial Ports of Entry Along the U.S.-Mexico Border 4

Figure 2: Truck Inspection Space at the World Trade Bridge,
Laredo, Texas 13

Figure 3: California State Truck Inspection Facility at Otay Mesa
With Covered Inspection Bays 15

Figure 4: Permanent Inspection Facility Staff in Calexico,
California, Select Trucks for Inspection 15

Abbreviations

CVSA	Commercial Vehicle Safety Alliance
DOT	Department of Transportation
EPA	Environmental Protection Agency
FMCSA	Federal Motor Carrier Safety Administration
GSA	General Services Administration
LTSS	Land Transportation Standards Subcommittee
NAFTA	North American Free Trade Agreement

GAO
Accountability * Integrity * Reliability

United States General Accounting Office
Washington, DC 20548

December 21, 2001

The Honorable John D. Dingell
Ranking Minority Member
Committee on Energy and Commerce
House of Representatives

The Honorable James L. Oberstar
Ranking Democratic Member
Committee on Transportation and Infrastructure
House of Representatives

The Honorable Edolphus Towns
Ranking Minority Member
Subcommittee on Commerce, Trade, and Consumer Protection
Committee on Energy and Commerce
House of Representatives

The Honorable Robert A. Borski
Ranking Democratic Member
Subcommittee on Highways and Transit
Committee on Transportation and Infrastructure
House of Representatives

As part of the North American Free Trade Agreement (NAFTA), commercial trucks from Mexico were to be allowed to travel throughout the United States beginning in January 2000. Because of concerns about the safety of these vehicles, the United States has limited Mexican truck operations to commercial zones near the border. In February 2001, a NAFTA arbitration panel ruled that the United States' blanket refusal to process applications by Mexican trucking companies to provide cross-border services beyond the commercial zones violated its NAFTA obligations. The panel noted, however, that the United States could require Mexican motor carriers to meet U.S. safety requirements. In February 2001, the administration announced that it would give Mexican trucks access to all U.S. highways by January 2002. The Department of Transportation and Related Agencies Appropriations Act for Fiscal Year 2002, enacted in December 2001, provided increased funding for safety activities related to Mexican motor carriers and set forth a series of requirements that the Department of Transportation (DOT) must meet before Mexican trucks can travel beyond the commercial zones.

In response to your concerns about the safety of Mexican trucks, we examined (1) the extent to which Mexican-domiciled commercial trucks are likely to travel beyond the U.S. border commercial zones once the border is fully opened, (2) U.S. government agencies' efforts to ensure that Mexican commercial carriers meet U.S. safety and emissions standards, and (3) how Mexican government and private sector efforts contribute to ensuring that Mexican commercial vehicles entering the United States meet U.S. safety and emissions standards. To address these objectives, we met with and obtained documents from a wide variety of officials from the U.S. and Mexican governments and industry representatives. (See app. I for a detailed discussion of how we conducted our work.)

Results in Brief

Relatively few Mexican carriers are expected to initially operate beyond the commercial zones once the United States fully opens its highways to Mexican carriers. Specific regulatory and economic factors that may limit the number of Mexican carriers operating beyond the commercial zones include: (1) the lack of established business relationships beyond the U.S. commercial zones that would permit drivers to return to Mexico carrying cargo, (2) difficulties obtaining competitively priced insurance, (3) congestion and delays in crossing the U.S.-Mexico border that make long-haul operations less profitable, and (4) high registration fees. Over time, improvements in trucking and border operations may increase the number of Mexican commercial vehicles traveling beyond the commercial zones. For example, innovations such as automated clearance systems could reduce the need for time-consuming paperwork reviews at the border.

The Department of Transportation does not have a fully developed or approved operational plan in conjunction with border states to ensure that Mexican-domiciled carriers comply with U.S. safety standards. The Department has not secured permanent space at any of the 25 southwest border ports of entry where commercial trucks enter the United States, and, at present, only the state of California has established permanent inspection facilities. The Department also has not completed agreements with border states on how 58 federal inspectors (projected to increase to 141 in fiscal year 2002) and 89 state inspectors (some of whom work part-time) will share inspection responsibilities along the border. States are responsible for ensuring that Mexican trucks adhere to U.S. emissions standards. California is the only southwest border state with a truck emissions inspection program in place at the border—testing is conducted at two of its four commercial ports of entry. In addition to these infrastructure and personnel challenges, the fiscal year 2002 DOT appropriations act establishes new requirements for DOT. These include deploying advanced technology to weigh trucks, requiring the electronic verification of Mexican commercial drivers' licenses, and ensuring that staff and adequate space are available for truck inspections. These additional requirements highlight the importance of having an approved operational plan and timeline.

While the Mexican government has developed truck safety regulations and taken steps to enforce safety and air emissions standards, these efforts are relatively recent and it is thus too early to assess their effectiveness. With DOT's support, Mexico has developed five databases with important information on the safety records of its commercial drivers and motor carriers. However, as of October 2001, the commercial driver's license database covered less than one-quarter of Mexico's commercial drivers. Mexico has also participated in NAFTA-related efforts to make motor carrier safety regulations compatible across the three member nations. Apart from government efforts, Mexican private sector and industry groups also report conducting activities to improve the safety of Mexican commercial vehicles.

This report contains a recommendation that DOT develop and implement a coordinated operational plan for truck safety at the southwest border. This plan should include reaching agreements with the border states and other federal agencies on space, staffing, day-to-day operations, and a timetable for when these actions will occur. DOT officials agreed with our recommendation. However, they strongly emphasized that they were well advanced in their efforts to fulfill our recommendation as well as respond to the requirements contained in DOT's fiscal year 2002 appropriations act. We disagree with DOT's comments that they are well advanced in their efforts to implement our recommendation as well as the many requirements contained in the appropriations act. Even prior to the act, DOT had not reached agreements with the states on how to allocate their inspectors or with other federal agencies on the space needed to conduct additional truck inspections.

Background

Since NAFTA's implementation, trade between the United States and Mexico has more than doubled, growing from $100 billion in 1994 to $248 billion in 2000.[1] Enhanced trade has increased the number of northbound

---

[1] NAFTA was agreed to by Canada, Mexico, and the United States in 1992 and implemented in 1994.

truck crossings from 2.7 million in fiscal year 1994 to more than 4.3 million in fiscal year 2001. According to DOT, about 80,000 trucks crossed the border in fiscal year 2000, 63,000 of which were estimated to be of Mexican origin. Trucks from Mexico enter the United States at border crossing points in four U.S. states (see fig. 1), but most of the crossings occurred at five ports of entry in fiscal year 2001: Laredo, El Paso, Hidalgo/Pharr in Texas, and Calexico and Otay Mesa in California.

Figure 1: Commercial Ports of Entry Along the U.S.-Mexico Border

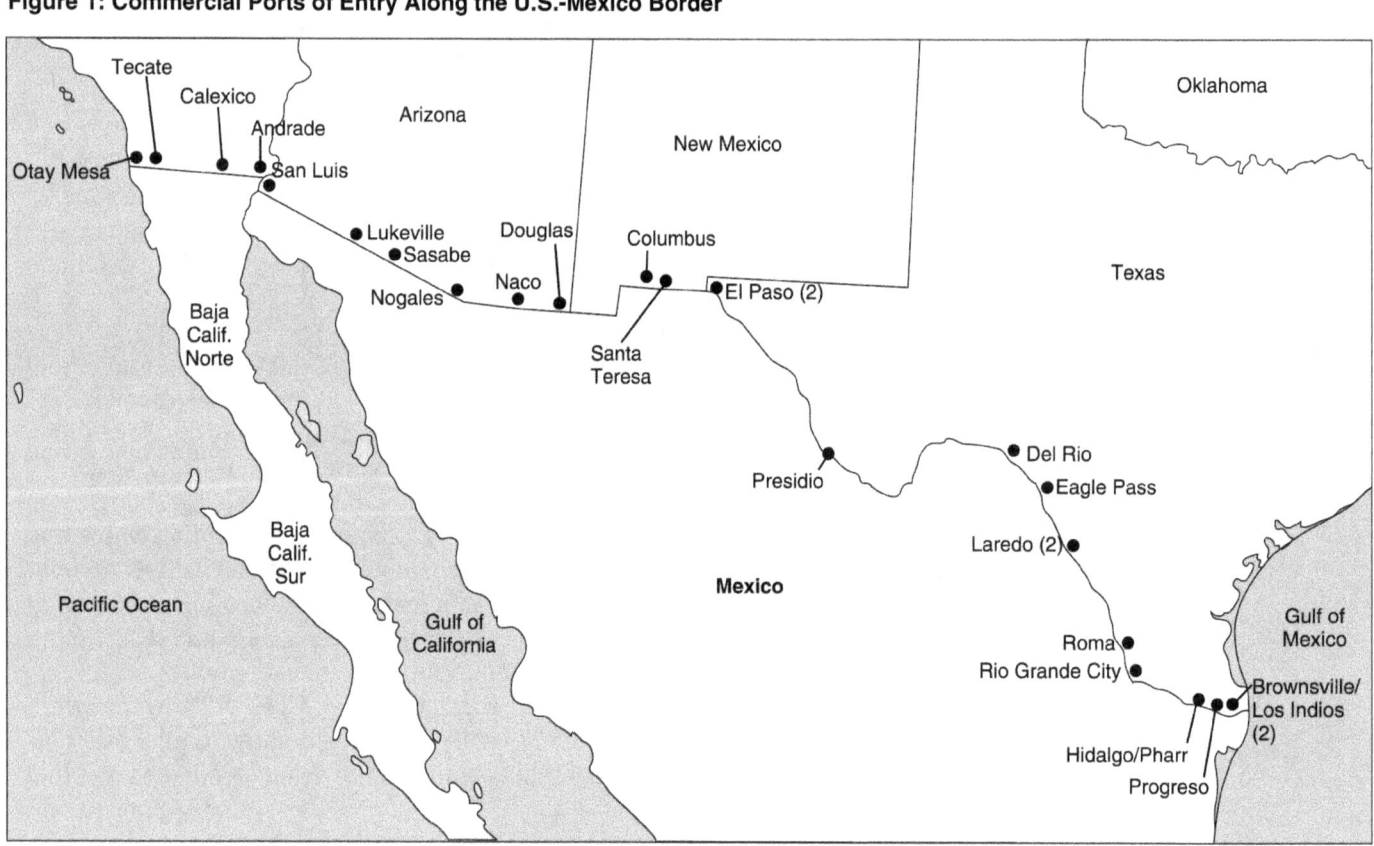

Note: Numbers in parenthesis indicate the number of ports of entry for those with more than one.

Source: GSA and DOT.

Commercial truck traffic at Texas and California ports of entry, which handle approximately 91 percent of truck crossings from Mexico, has grown just over 60 percent since NAFTA went into effect. Table 1 lists the principal commercial ports of entry and the number of truck crossings that occurred at each port in fiscal year 2001.

Table 1: Truck Crossings From Mexico Into the United States, Fiscal Year 2001

Location	Truck crossings	Percentage of total crossings
Texas		
Laredo	1,419,165	33%
El Paso	656,257	15
Hidalgo/Pharr	367,991	9
Brownsville	255,231	6
All others	223,159	5
Total Texas	**2,921,803**	**68**
California		
Otay Mesa	700,453	16
Calexico	259,174	6
All others	63,970	1
Total California	**1,023,597**	**23**
Arizona		
Nogales	251,474	6
All others	90,424	2
Total Arizona	**341,898**	**8**
New Mexico	**34,851**	**1**
Total	4,322,149	100%

Source: U.S. Customs Service.

Under NAFTA, barriers have gradually been reduced for trade in goods and services among Canada, Mexico, and the United States. Among other things, NAFTA allows Mexican commercial vehicles greater access to U.S. highways to facilitate trade between the two countries. Under NAFTA's original timeline, Mexico and the United States agreed to permit commercial trucks to operate within both countries' border states no later than December 18, 1995, and beyond the border states by January 1, 2000.[2]

However, due to U.S. concerns about the safety of Mexican trucks and the adequacy of Mexico's truck safety regulatory system, the United States postponed implementation of NAFTA's cross-border trucking provisions and only permitted Mexican trucks to continue to operate in designated commercial zones within Arizona, California, New Mexico, and Texas.[3]

---

[2] Canada and the United States have permitted each other's trucks complete access to all highways since 1982.

[3] Commercial zones are designated areas where Mexican commercial vehicles are allowed to (1) transfer their cargo to U.S. carriers or (2) unload their cargo for later pick-up by U.S. carriers. Commercial zones generally encompass areas extending between 3 and 20 miles north of U.S. border cities.

DOT's Office of Inspector General and GAO have reported that out-of-service rates for Mexican trucks operating in the commercial zones exceeded those of U.S. trucks in the nation as a whole. The Inspector General has also reported that the percentage of Mexican trucks placed out-of-service in the commercial zones declined from 44 percent in fiscal year 1997 to 36 percent in fiscal year 2000.

In 1998, Mexico challenged the United States' delay in implementing NAFTA's schedule for cross-border trucking. In February 2001, a NAFTA arbitration panel ruled that the United States' blanket refusal to review and consider Mexican motor carrier applications for operating authority to provide cross-border trucking services beyond the commercial zones violated its NAFTA obligations. The panel indicated that under NAFTA, the United States is permitted to establish its own safety standards and ensure that Mexican trucking firms and drivers comply with U.S. safety and operating regulations. However, the panel also noted that due to differing regulatory regimes in each country, the United States need not treat Mexican carriers or drivers exactly the same as those from the United States or Canada, provided that such different treatment is imposed in good faith with respect to a legitimate safety concern and conforms with relevant NAFTA provisions.

In February 2001, the administration announced that it would comply with its NAFTA obligations and allow Mexican commercial carriers to operate beyond the commercial zones by January 2002. In May 2001, DOT issued three proposed rules that would revise existing regulations and application forms and establish a two-tiered application process for Mexican carriers seeking authority to operate within and beyond the commercial zones.[4] Under the proposed rules, a carrier's authority would be conditioned on satisfactory completion of a safety audit within 18 months of receiving conditional operating authority.[5] According to the Federal Motor Carrier Safety Administration (FMCSA), the agency primarily responsible for enforcing U.S. truck safety regulations, the final regulations would ensure that FMCSA receives adequate information to assess an applicant's safety program and its ability to comply with U.S. safety standards before it is

---

[4]Among other things, the rules would require carriers to (1) describe their operations, (2) self-certify that they understand and will comply with U.S. safety standards, and (3) describe their recordkeeping procedures relating to drivers and accidents.

[5]These safety audits are expected to focus on reviewing a carrier's records and not individual truck inspections.

authorized to operate in the United States.[6] As of December 2001, DOT had not finalized these rules. DOT officials said these rules were not finalized because the Department was waiting for the outcome of the congressional appropriations process. Additional statutory requirements that must be met before Mexican commercial trucks can travel beyond the commercial zones are contained in the fiscal year 2002 DOT appropriations act. These include a range of inspection requirements and facility enhancements, such as adding weigh-in-motion scales at the 10 highest volume crossings. Additional requirements are discussed later in this report.

Relatively Few Mexican Carriers Initially Expected Beyond Border Commercial Zones

U.S. border state and Mexican transportation officials and representatives of U.S. and Mexican trucking organizations we interviewed said they believe few Mexican carriers will initially apply for authority to travel beyond the commercial zones. Further, they suggested that any increase in truck traffic would be gradual. As of October 2001, fewer than 200 Mexican trucking companies had applied to DOT to operate in the United States beyond the border commercial zones.[7] Regulatory and economic factors may affect Mexican trucking companies' interest and ability to operate vehicles beyond the commercial zones in the short run, but long-term trends in cross-border trade operations could increase interest in operating beyond the commercial zones.

Regulatory and Economic Factors May Limit Mexican Carriers' Willingness to Seek Access Beyond the Commercial Zones

A number of regulatory and economic factors may limit the number of Mexican carriers operating beyond the commercial zones in the near term. For example, U.S. and Mexican officials identified the lack of established business relationships in the United States as a factor likely to reduce the number of Mexican trucking companies willing to operate beyond the commercial zones. According to U.S. and Mexican officials, many Mexican trucking companies lack distribution ties outside the commercial zones and thus do not have immediate access to "backhaul" cargo from the

---

[6]FMCSA's responsibilities include: ensuring that eligible foreign motor carriers operating in the United States comply with U.S. federal motor carrier safety regulations; promoting information exchange regarding truck safety among the NAFTA countries by providing U.S. enforcement personnel the capability to verify information on foreign carriers, drivers, and vehicles; granting authority to Mexican carriers to operate in the United States; and enforcing compliance.

[7]More than three-fourths of these applications were made in 1996 and 1997. Mexican officials and FMCSA have concluded that Mexican carriers stopped applying for operating authority once they realized that the United States was not processing applications to operate beyond the commercial zones.

United States to Mexico that would allow them to operate profitably. The officials noted that it would take time to develop these business relationships.

The cost and availability of insurance may also affect the number of Mexican carriers operating beyond the commercial zones. According to the National Association of Independent Insurers, newly established trucking companies and Mexican trucking companies wanting to operate beyond the commercial zones face a competitive disadvantage in obtaining affordable insurance. According to companies currently providing insurance to Mexican trucking companies and an insurance industry representative, premiums for Mexican trucking companies will initially be set at the highest level and gradually decline as the market matures. These individuals stated that it would take time for the insurance industry to become familiar with the financial and safety records of Mexican companies and drivers and to develop effective means to access information for underwriting purposes. Further, large U.S.-based and multinational insurers are likely to gradually enter the Mexican market as demand for insurance in the Mexican trucking industry increases. The number of U.S.-based firms currently providing insurance coverage for Mexican trucks entering the United States is unknown. According to insurance company officials, fewer than 10 U.S. firms may be providing insurance for daily trips into the United States by Mexican trucking companies.

Also, according to Mexican private industry representatives and U.S. researchers, congestion and delays in crossing the U.S.-Mexico border result in added operating costs for Mexican carriers. These costs make it less profitable to use newer, more expensive vehicles to wait in lines at the border. Mexican government and private sector officials stated that delays in crossing the border have increased since the terrorist attacks on September 11, 2001. These delays could limit long-haul operations and encourage further reliance on the existing cross-border shuttle (drayage) system.[8]

Like other carriers, Mexican carriers must pay registration fees to each state in which they operate in the United States. The International Registration Plan was created to facilitate the payment and reduce the

---

[8]Drayage trucks provide shuttle freight service within the commercial zones on both sides of the border.

cost of these fees by allowing one member state to collect registration fees and distribute them to other jurisdictions as necessary. However, Mexico is not a member of the plan so Mexican companies must instead purchase individual trip permits for each state in which they travel.[9] According to an International Registration Plan representative, since these individual trip permits cost more in the aggregate, Mexican carriers could be at a competitive disadvantage. For example, a Mexican truck traveling from Nuevo Laredo, Mexico, to Tulsa, Oklahoma, must purchase trip permits before traveling through Texas and Oklahoma. Table 2 depicts the costs for an International Registration Plan member and a non-member traveling through these states once a week for a year. As seen in table 2, a non-member truck would pay about $5,600 more annually than a member truck.

Table 2: Registration Fees for International Registration Plan Members and Non-members

	Registration fees assessed by each state[a]	
	Member truck	Non-member truck
Texas	$588	$5,200
Oklahoma	$303	$1,248
Total	**$891 per year**	**$6,448 per year**

[a]Based on an 80,000 pound gross weight truck traveling round-trip once per week for one year between Nuevo Laredo, Mexico, and Tulsa, Oklahoma

Source: GAO analysis based on International Registration Plan data.

According to an American Trucking Associations official, a medium-term solution for Mexican trucking companies to take advantage of the cost savings and convenience associated with the International Registration Plan would be to register in a state that is a plan member. A Mexican trucking company may participate in the International Registration Plan by selecting a member state and establishing a business presence such as a sales or service office in that state. However, establishing such a presence may entail additional costs such as federal and state taxes. When we discussed these registration fees and potential taxes with Mexican public and private officials in October 2001, they were unaware that they needed to pay them. In commenting on a draft of this report, DOT officials said

---

[9]Not all states issue individual trip permits. For example, California requires an annual registration fee for non-members of the International Registration Plan.

they have discussed these registration fees with Mexican government officials.

The small scale and size of Mexican trucking operations could also limit travel beyond the commercial zones. Mexico's truck fleet is relatively small compared with that of the United States, and Mexican trucking association representatives said that their members' fleets have fewer trucks than their U.S. counterparts. For example, there are nearly 600,000 trucking companies with approximately 6.3 million tractors and trailers in the United States, according to DOT. Mexico, in contrast, in 2000[10] had approximately 83,000 federally registered commercial cargo carriers with approximately 277,000 tractors and trailers (trucks may also be registered by Mexican states if they do not drive on federal highways).[11] Further, the overall age of the Mexican commercial vehicle fleet may also limit the number of Mexican carriers able to operate beyond the commercial zones. According to Mexican registration data, in 2000 only 20 percent of the commercial cargo trucks registered for use on Mexican federal highways were manufactured after 1994. Mexican industry officials told us that trucks manufactured in Mexico prior to this date were not built to U.S. safety and emissions standards. Mexican carriers can apply to have older vehicles certified to be in compliance with U.S. safety standards. However, Mexican industry officials told us that these vehicles might have difficulties meeting U.S. emissions standards.

Uncertainty about DOT's final rules for obtaining operating authority has reduced the number of Mexican carriers that will initially apply for authority to operate beyond the commercial zones, according to Mexican government and private sector representatives. According to these officials, this uncertainty makes it difficult to plan for the future since union contracts allowing travel beyond the commercial zones and distribution ties must be established in advance.

---

[10]Secretariat of Communication and Transportation, *Estadistica Basica del Autotransporte Federal.* (Mexico City, Mexico: 2000).

[11]An additional 23,000 vehicles of all types are operated by private trucking companies. Private trucking companies own and operate their own fleet.

GAO-02-238 NAFTA Commercial Trucking

Increased Efficiency in Trucking and Border Operations Is Needed Before a Rise in Long-haul Commercial Vehicle Operations Will Occur

Cross-border trucking beyond the commercial zones may increase as firms seek to eliminate inefficiencies associated with the current system of drayage operations. Restrictions on cross-border commercial vehicle traffic have led to a transport system that typically requires three tractors and/or trailers to carry goods from the interior of Mexico to the U.S. interior. For example, a long-haul vehicle is used to bring cargo to the Mexican border from an interior Mexican state, where it is transferred to a short-haul drayage truck that moves the goods across the U.S. border into the commercial zones. To carry a shipment beyond the commercial zones, it must be transferred to a third vehicle domiciled in the United States. This system is cumbersome and inefficient, according to the Office of the U.S. Trade Representative, trucking industry representatives, businesses, and academic researchers. For example, as we reported previously, nearly half of the containers crossing the border from Mexico into the United States in 1998 were empty because they left products or raw materials in Mexico—yet still had to be processed by U.S. Customs.[12] According to U.S. industry representatives and researchers, the time required to complete transfers within the border commercial zones hinders the "just-in-time" nature of many assembly plants (maquiladoras) and agricultural industries, and can result in additional costs. They note that a single-truck transport system would be more efficient, practical, and less costly. In addition, government officials who monitor hazardous materials shipments contend that minimizing transfers and the handling of these loads would decrease the risk of dangerous accidents and spills.

According to researchers and Mexican government officials, technological and other innovations, such as an automated clearance system requiring carriers to provide documentation electronically, would also encourage the development of cross-border trucking beyond the commercial zones by reducing the need for time-consuming paperwork reviews at the border. According to Mexican customs officials, new programs, such as the U.S. Customs Service's Business Anti-Smuggling Coalition, could encourage the growth of such cross-border trucking by reducing the time spent waiting in lines at the border.[13]

---

[12]See *U.S.-Mexico Border: Better Planning, Coordination Needed to Handle Growing Commercial Traffic* (GAO/NSIAD-00-25, Mar. 3, 2000).

[13]The Business Anti-Smuggling Coalition is a business-led, U.S. Customs-supported initiative created to combat narcotics smuggling via commercial trade.

The United States and Most U.S. Border States Are Not Prepared to Ensure That Mexican Commercial Carriers Meet U.S. Safety Standards

DOT faces a number of challenges in implementing a coordinated truck safety system—including acquiring adequate infrastructure and deploying personnel—at the U.S.-Mexico border.[14] Few permanent facilities are in place for truck safety inspections and DOT only began taking steps to secure its own space for these inspections in August 2001. It also has not fully integrated its inspection personnel and their activities with those of the border states. With regard to emissions inspections, the Environmental Protection Agency (EPA) relies on state governments to establish and apply their own enforcement procedures. These operational challenges must be reconciled with a number of new requirements contained in the fiscal year 2002 DOT appropriations act.

Few Permanent Truck Safety Inspection Facilities Exist at U.S. Southwest Border Ports of Entry

Although we reported in 1997 and 2000 that FMCSA needs to be more proactive in securing inspection facilities at planned or existing border installations, the agency only began taking steps to secure its own space in August 2001 and has been occupying temporary space provided by Customs without the benefit of interagency agreements.[15] Currently, only 2 of 25 commercial ports of entry have permanent inspection facilities—both are state facilities in California. Other state facilities are being constructed or planned in the other three border states. However, federal and state officials have not formally agreed on how federal and state facilities will complement each other.

Permanent truck inspection facilities allow for more rigorous inspections, provide scales and measuring devices to screen trucks for weight and size, protect inspectors from the extreme heat prevalent at the border, and signal a commitment to enforce truck safety standards. At the three states without permanent facilities—Texas, Arizona, and New Mexico—Customs typically allows state and federal truck safety inspections on the agency's property on a temporary basis; however, if capacity is reached for storing trucks placed out-of-service, inspectors are unable to conduct additional safety inspections (app. II describes the amount of space designated for

---

[14]FMCSA and the border states have worked with the Mexican government, carriers, and industry associations to develop an enhanced commercial carrier safety regime and help carriers understand U.S. safety standards. These actions are discussed in the following section.

[15]See *U.S.-Mexico Border: Better Planning, Coordination Needed to Handle Growing Commercial Traffic* (GAO/NSIAD-00-25, Mar. 3, 2000) and *Commercial Trucking: Safety Concerns about Mexican Trucks Remain Even as Inspection Activity Increases* (GAO/RCED-97-68, Apr. 9, 1997).

truck inspection activities at southwest border ports of entry). For example, the Laredo, Texas, ports of entry handle the greatest number of northbound trucks, accounting for approximately 33 percent of all northbound commercial traffic. In Laredo, Customs has designated space for 33 trucks to be inspected or placed out-of-service, yet according to the U.S. Customs port director in Laredo, approximately 5,500 to 6,100 trucks cross at the two Laredo ports on an average day.[16] As fig. 2 shows, spaces used by federal truck safety inspectors at the World Trade Bridge in Laredo are not covered, nor is there lighting available for inspectors to conduct safety inspections at night.

Figure 2: Truck Inspection Space at the World Trade Bridge, Laredo, Texas

In light of the limited amount of temporary space for truck inspection activities, FMCSA has recently begun to take steps to acquire its own space in anticipation of increasing border enforcement personnel. FMCSA submitted its space needs for border port of entry facilities to the General Services Administration (GSA) in August 2001 in an attempt to secure space at federal ports of entry.[17] However, it is not clear when or if inspection space at these facilities can be acquired. According to a GSA

---

[16]The port of entry facilities in Laredo include the World Trade Border Station and the Colombia Border Station.

[17]GSA either owns or leases the commercial port of entry facilities to federal agencies working at the southwest border.

official, GSA and Customs must first conduct site surveys to determine the amount of vacant space available at port of entry facilities for truck inspections. As a result of heightened security in response to the September 11, 2001, terrorist attacks on the United States, Customs is reassessing its space needs at these facilities, with important implications for truck inspection activities. In discussions among FMCSA, GSA, and Customs held in October 2001, Customs said it will no longer allow trucks placed out-of-service for safety violations to remain on Customs compounds due to safety concerns related to allowing mechanics and tow truck operators on the compound. [18] Instead, federal and state inspectors must escort these vehicles off the facility. For example, in Texas a tow truck meets out-of-service vehicles at the Customs gate and tows them off the compound. A FMCSA official in Texas said these vehicles are rarely towed to Mexico unless they are empty. It is unclear what effect this development will have on the number and type of truck inspections that can be conducted in both the near and long term at federal ports of entry.

As noted, only 2 of the 25 commercial ports of entry have permanent truck inspection facilities—both state-operated facilities located in California. As permanent facilities dedicated to truck safety inspections, they have space to perform inspections and to place vehicles out-of-service (see figs. 3 and 4).

---

[18]The U.S. Customs Service is responsible for ensuring compliance with trade regulations and contraband/drug interdiction at border ports of entry.

Figure 3: California State Truck Inspection Facility at Otay Mesa With Covered Inspection Bays

Figure 4: Permanent Inspection Facility Staff in Calexico, California, Select Trucks for Inspection

Note: A California Highway Patrol observer visually inspects vehicles to determine if they should be more thoroughly inspected and obtains weight data from weigh-in-motion scales.

The three border states without permanent truck inspection facilities at border ports of entry—Texas, Arizona, and New Mexico—are planning to build facilities at some crossings. To construct truck safety inspection facilities, DOT officials said they plan to make the following allocations based on the fiscal year 2002 DOT appropriations act: $12 million for Texas, $54 million to be divided among the four border states, and $2.3 million for federal facility improvements. Texas plans to build eight permanent truck safety inspection facilities that would be adjacent to the Customs ports of entry.[19] The facilities would be similar in function to California's truck inspection facilities. City officials in Laredo and El Paso, however, object to the facilities being so close to the border, arguing that these facilities would interfere with the flow of commerce. Local opposition to placing truck inspection facilities at the border and constraints on state funding have impeded progress. State officials estimate that the permanent facilities will not be completed until 2004.

In the interim, Texas has established one temporary truck inspection site in El Paso directly adjacent to a federal port of entry facility and began inspecting trucks there in July 2001. Texas also plans to establish four other temporary truck inspection sites directly adjacent to port of entry facilities in Laredo, Eagle Pass, Pharr, and Brownsville. The state plans to lease or purchase 5 acres of land for each of these temporary sites and provide a trailer for office space. As of November 2001, state officials had not implemented plans for the four temporary truck inspection sites.

Arizona and New Mexico have each begun work on a permanent truck inspection facility. In 1998, Arizona acquired a 10-acre lot adjacent to Customs' port of entry in Nogales on which to construct a permanent truck inspection facility. According to Arizona officials, this project is scheduled for completion in 2002. New Mexico has also started construction of a truck inspection facility in Santa Teresa. According to New Mexico officials, funding is currently available only for the groundwork. Further construction will not be scheduled until funding is available to complete the facility.

---

[19]Two facilities each are planned for Brownsville, Laredo, and El Paso, and one each in Pharr/McAllen and Eagle Pass.

DOT Is Increasing the Number of Safety Inspection Personnel But Has Not Integrated Its Efforts With the Border States

According to DOT officials, the fiscal year 2002 DOT appropriations act provides funding to hire and train additional federal and state safety inspection personnel. However, federal and state officials have not yet agreed on the level of staffing needed at temporary and permanent truck inspection facilities to achieve safety goals. For example, in Texas, there are no formal agreements between the state and FMCSA about coordinating inspection responsibilities at the ports of entry, or agreements establishing the number of federal and state inspection personnel at the proposed temporary and permanent sites. As of October 2001, there were 58 federal officials inspecting trucks on the southwest border. FMCSA officials said that $9.9 million in fiscal year 2002 funding would permit them to increase the number of enforcement personnel at ports of entry to 141. In addition, FMCSA will also use these funds to hire 134 staff who will perform safety audits and conduct compliance reviews of Mexican motor carriers seeking authority to operate beyond the commercial zones. The appropriations act requires that 50 percent of these safety audits and compliance reviews be conducted "on-site." Mexican officials stated that they would only allow these reviews within their country in the presence of a Mexican inspector.

As of October 2001, the 4 border states had assigned 89 inspectors to border crossings to inspect trucks entering the United States from Mexico—43 in Texas, 41 in California, 3 in Arizona, and 2 in New Mexico.[20] The fiscal year 2002 DOT appropriations act also provided $18 million for the border states to hire truck safety inspectors. Prior to passage of the act, Arizona planned to add a total of 11 inspectors and New Mexico planned to add a total of 9 inspectors in 2002 and 2003. Texas did not plan to increase the number of its inspectors until federal and state funds were committed to build inspection facilities. California was unsure how budgetary considerations would change its staffing levels.

---

[20]Staffing levels reflect the number of inspectors assigned to facilities and do not represent full-time equivalents. In California, inspectors have been permanently assigned to the truck inspection facilities. In contrast, inspectors in the other border states are not permanently assigned to ports of entry and devote only a portion of their time to truck safety inspections at the ports of entry. In Laredo, Texas, for example, state troopers inspect trucks at the two commercial ports of entry approximately 20 hours a week.

Emissions Inspections of Commercial Trucks Vary by State

Under the 1990 Clean Air Act, EPA is required to establish minimum national standards for air pollution and individual states are assigned primary responsibility to ensure compliance with the standards through state implementation plans. Such plans can include truck emissions inspections. Since 1994, EPA's primary role in regulating commercial truck emissions has been to certify compliance of commercial truck engines at the factories where they are manufactured. EPA relies on the commercial truck engine manufacturers to certify that their products meet air emissions standards and conducts spot checks at engine factories.

Some U.S. states have implemented emissions testing requirements for heavy-duty diesel trucks as part of their efforts to meet EPA air quality standards for non-attainment areas.[21] State testing programs differ significantly, with some states requiring yearly checks of trucks and others operating both annual and more frequent roadside inspection programs. California, which has a large number of areas that do not meet federal air quality standards, including the state's two southern border counties, conducts emissions tests at the border. Since 1999, California has assigned two inspectors each to the ports of entry at Calexico and Otay Mesa to monitor the emissions of U.S. and Mexican heavy-duty vehicles. According to California state officials, in 2000, the failure rate for U.S. trucks was approximately 8 percent, while the failure rate for Mexican trucks was 12 percent.

Arizona also operates an emissions testing program for commercial trucks, but testing is conducted on a yearly basis for trucks registered in the state's two non-attainment areas, Phoenix and Tucson—neither of which are located at the border. Neither Texas nor New Mexico performs emissions inspections at the border.

Meeting New Statutory Requirements for Southwest Border Truck Safety Inspections Will Require Additional Planning and Coordination

The fiscal year 2002 DOT appropriations act provides increased funding for activities related to the safety of Mexican carriers and sets forth a number of new requirements that DOT must meet before Mexican motor carriers can be granted authority to operate beyond the commercial zones. Meeting these requirements could entail significant operational and facility planning by DOT in coordination with the border states and other federal agencies. DOT officials said in December 2001 they are unsure when they

---

[21]EPA defines a non-attainment area as a geographical region that exceeds scientifically accepted levels for certain air pollutants.

will be able to meet the requirements and fully open the border given the short time these requirements have been in place. Among other things, DOT must

- equip all U.S.-Mexico commercial border crossings with scales suitable for enforcement action. Five of the 10 highest volume crossings must have weigh-in-motion scales, and the remaining 5 highest volume crossings must have such scales within 12 months;
- require federal and state inspectors to electronically verify the status and validity of the license of each Mexican commercial driver transporting certain quantities of hazardous materials, drivers undergoing specified inspections, and at least 50 percent of other Mexican commercial drivers;
- require Mexican commercial trucks to cross into the United States only where there is a safety inspector on duty and adequate capacity exists to conduct a sufficient number of meaningful safety inspections and accommodate out-of-service trucks; and
- require Level I inspections and Commercial Vehicle Safety Alliance (CVSA) [22] decals for all Mexican commercial vehicles that wish to operate beyond the commercial zones but do not display such decals.[23]

DOT's Plans to Assess Compliance with U.S. Safety Standards

According to FMCSA's Associate Administrator for Enforcement and Program Delivery, FMCSA plans to measure the progress of Mexican carriers in complying with U.S. safety standards by using truck out-of-service rates, traffic fatality rates, and accident rates. FMCSA's goal will be for Mexican carriers' rates to be comparable to those for U.S.-domiciled carriers. Currently, available data do not permit differentiating between drayage (cross-border shuttle) and long-haul carriers operating at the border. Differentiating between these two classes of vehicles in terms of calculating out-of-service rates will be important in determining the extent to which the safety goals are being met.

---

[22] CVSA is a non-profit organization of federal, state, and provincial government agencies and representatives from private industry in the United States, Canada, and Mexico dedicated to improving commercial vehicle safety. According to FMCSA officials, only law enforcement personnel can affix CVSA decals. CVSA decals are issued when a vehicle passes either a Level I or a Level V inspection. A Level I inspection consists of an examination of both the driver and vehicle. A Level V inspection includes all of the steps involved in a Level I inspection, except for an inspection of the driver. The decals are valid for a 3-month period.

[23] This excludes Mexican motor carriers that have been granted permanent operating authority for 3 consecutive years from this provision.

Mexico Has Taken Steps to Improve Commercial Vehicle Safety and Emissions, But Extent of Compliance With U.S. Standards Remains Unclear

The Mexican government has developed truck safety regulations and reports taking steps to enforce safety and air emissions standards but these efforts are relatively recent and it is too early to assess their effectiveness. With support from DOT, it has also developed key databases related to commercial vehicle safety and it has participated in trinational efforts to make U.S., Canadian, and Mexican land transportation standards more compatible. Some Mexican private sector and industry groups have also made efforts to improve the safety of Mexican commercial vehicles by implementing safety programs and purchasing new vehicles.

Mexico Has Begun Implementing New Safety and Emissions Standards

Mexico has developed new regulations establishing specifications for vehicle safety equipment, transportation of hazardous goods, vehicle inspection standards, and maximum limits for emissions of certain chemicals. According to Mexican officials, prior to 1992, Mexico had few vehicle manufacturing and operating safety standards, and those that did exist were very general. Since 1992, Mexico has developed and implemented specific federal regulations dealing with commercial vehicle safety. These include regulations establishing specifications for buses, license plates, vehicle weights, and dimensions. Mexico has also created operating safety standards, including speed limits for commercial motor vehicles. According to DOT, Mexico is considering implementing additional vehicle manufacturing standards, which could be modeled after U.S. or European standards.

In addition, Mexico has developed and implemented standards related to the transportation of hazardous goods. These standards address labeling, classifying, inspecting, documenting, storing, and shipping hazardous goods. According to DOT and Mexican officials, the standards are based on the United Nations Recommendations on the Transport of Dangerous Goods.

In July 2000, Mexico finalized its first regulation establishing the criteria and authority for roadside commercial vehicle inspections. According to CVSA and Mexican officials, this regulation is modeled after the CVSA inspection procedures and out-of-service criteria. The regulation establishes the procedures used by federal officials for inspecting commercial vehicles and placing them out-of-service. It also establishes a time frame for inspecting these vehicles, ranging from 20 minutes for buses and commercial vehicles carrying hazardous materials to 30 minutes for commercial vehicles carrying general cargo. According to Mexican officials, prior to July 2001 when the regulation was fully implemented, there were no rules for placing commercial vehicles out-of-service and only the most serious violations would have resulted in putting a vehicle out-of-service.

Mexico has also developed and implemented standards limiting commercial vehicle emissions. These standards establish limits for air emissions of hydrocarbons, carbon monoxide, nitrous oxide, and vehicle smoke from new diesel engines. They also establish limits for vehicle smoke for diesel engines in use, as well as a program for inspecting diesel emissions. According to Mexican officials, commercial vehicles are subject to emissions inspections every 6 months.

Mexico's Commercial Vehicle Inspection Personnel and Activities

Mexico's commercial vehicle inspections are performed by 350 inspectors from the Secretariat for Communication and Transportation—the agency primarily responsible for inspecting commercial vehicles traveling on federal highways. In addition, 5,000 inspectors from the Federal Preventive Police have been trained to conduct inspections.[24] Many of these inspectors were trained by U.S. border state inspectors. During 2000, Mexican inspectors performed a total of 114,138 roadside vehicle inspections and found 12,929 vehicles in violation of safety standards. In 1999, they conducted 88,490 roadside vehicle inspections and found 5,367 vehicles in violation of safety standards. Mexican federal inspectors also performed compliance reviews of motor carriers at their place of business, conducting 2,441 compliance reviews in 2000 and 1,003 in 1999.[25] While it is encouraging that the Mexican government is making efforts to inspect more commercial trucks, we have no information on the nature of the violations found or whether any sanctions or penalties may have been assessed for them. Further, as noted above, inspections conducted in 1999 and 2000 were not covered under Mexico's recently implemented (July 2001) commercial vehicle inspection regulations.

[24]According to Federal Preventive Police officials, police officers must observe a violation of traffic laws before stopping a vehicle to conduct a safety inspection. By contrast, Secretariat of Communication and Transportation inspectors have no such limitations.

[25]We were not able to determine the extent to which Mexico's compliance reviews are comparable to those done in the United States because we did not have the opportunity to observe these operations in either country.

According to the Secretariat of Communication and Transportation, Mexico plans to increase the percentage of commercial vehicles inspected each year, from 28 percent of the total fleet in 2000 to 50 percent in 2006. The 2001 program set the following minimum inspection activities and inspection-level goals:

- increase the total number of roadside inspections by 27 percent and the total number of carrier compliance reviews by 5 percent over 2000 levels;
- maintain a permanent enforcement presence in each of 10 main transportation corridors; and
- conduct 90 roadside inspections and 9 compliance reviews per year per inspector.

In June 2000, Mexico participated in the CVSA-sponsored "Roadcheck 2000" program, a trinational exercise carried out over a 3-day period with the United States and Canada. During this exercise, Mexican officials inspected a total of 1,428 Mexican commercial vehicles along federal highways, putting 246, or about 17 percent, out-of-service. However, as of October 2001, Mexico was not issuing CVSA decals. Mexican officials told us they were not issuing CVSA decals because the decals are not required by Mexican law.

Permanent Truck Inspection Facilities Modeled After California Facilities Planned

According to Mexican officials, Mexico is in the process of constructing 7 permanent truck inspection facilities similar to stations in California, with an additional 13 planned. All seven facilities under construction are to be completed by the end of 2001, with an additional six facilities scheduled for completion in 2002 and the remaining seven scheduled for completion in 2003. According to Mexican officials, three of these facilities—Mexicali, Matamoros, and Nuevo Laredo— are being constructed on highways leading to the border. The purpose of these stations, in part, is to inspect and weigh vehicles and thus reduce the number of accidents caused by overweight and unsafe commercial vehicles. According to Mexican officials, the stations will include weigh-in-motion scales and areas to inspect vehicles and remove noncompliant vehicles from circulation.

New Commercial Driver Training Requirements Planned

Mexican officials stated that they conducted a study to determine the factors causing accidents involving commercial vehicles. The study found that more than 80 percent of all accidents were caused by driver errors. To reduce the number of accidents, Mexico is developing and implementing new training requirements that would require each new commercial driver to receive a minimum of 420 hours of driver training, 70 percent of which constitutes instruction on the road. Drivers renewing their licenses would have to undergo 40 hours of instruction. This expanded training requirement is expected to be fully in place by 2005. Commercial vehicle drivers responsible for hazardous materials would need to meet additional requirements. At present, drivers can obtain commercial driver's licenses without such training.

Databases Constructed and Being Updated

Since NAFTA was signed, the Mexican government, with the assistance of FMCSA and TML, a private contractor, has developed and is adding information to several databases. These databases include (1) carrier and vehicle authorizations, (2) commercial driver's licenses, (3) accidents by Mexican commercial carriers and drivers, (4) results of inspections and audits, and (5) infractions. According to TML, it began working with Mexico to construct these databases in 1995. The databases are an integral piece of Mexico's motor carrier safety information system. While important for Mexico's internal purposes, they also provide information needed by U.S. law enforcement to verify driver and carrier information. Two of the five databases were available to U.S. law enforcement in 2000 and the remaining databases were to be available in 2001.

The first database, the Carrier and Vehicle Authorization Information System, was completed in 1998 to assist the Mexican government in issuing carrier operating authority permits, vehicle license plates, and vehicle highway permits. According to TML, as of June 2001, the database included all Mexican commercial cargo carriers registered with the federal government. According to Mexican government statistics from 2000, there are approximately 83,000 commercial cargo carriers comprising approximately 8,000 corporations and 75,000 sole-proprietorships. These carriers maintained about 372,000 vehicles of all types. U.S. federal inspectors have been able to access this database since October 2000. According to private sector officials, an estimated 75,000 other commercial trucks are registered in Mexican states and are not in this database. Mexican federal officials said that border drayage vehicles also would not be in the federal database since they do not travel on federal highways and thus are not subject to inspection by federal inspectors.

The second database, the Licencia Federal Information System, contains Mexican federal commercial driver's licenses.[26] It was completed in 1999

---

[26]We were not able to obtain data on the number of commercial driver's licenses issued by Mexican states.

to maintain records on commercial drivers and includes driver identification, license status, and medical certifications. According to TML, this database went on-line in January 2000, and as of December 2000, all 46 of Mexico's field offices issuing commercial driver's licenses had complete access to it. As of October 2001, 70,150, or 23 percent, of an estimated 300,000 federal commercial driver's licenses had been entered into the database. However, Mexican government officials say the database has information on 90 percent of the Mexican commercial drivers now crossing the border. Mexican government officials are entering records into this database as drivers renew their licenses and expect the database to contain all records by 2003. U.S. federal and state inspectors have been able to access this database since 2000. FMCSA policy requires that as of November 1, 2001, all Mexican commercial drivers entering the United States had to have a valid Mexican federal commercial driver's license in the database. If these drivers do not have a valid Mexican federal commercial driver's license in the database, FMCSA officials said they would be refused entry into the United States.

The third database, the Accident Reporting Information System, was completed in 2000 and records all accidents on Mexico's federal highways.[27] It includes an accident overview; vehicle, driver, and passenger identification; insurance information; information on damages; and other data. According to TML, phased implementation and interface with the United States were slated for completion by August 2001 but have been delayed because of the change of administrations in Mexico.

The fourth database, the Inspections and Audits Information System, was completed in 2000 to record the results of inspections and audits of motor carriers and their facilities. It includes inspection reports, as well as information on violations, infractions, and complaints. Mexican officials told us that these compliance reviews are conducted over a 15-day period. As of June 2001, there were 222 carrier audit records and 7,273 vehicle inspection records. We were unable to obtain information on what these inspections uncovered.

The fifth database, the Infraction Information System, was completed in 2000 to process and report infractions committed by Mexican vehicles and drivers on federal highways. Phased implementation of this database began in 2001. According to TML, as of June 2001, there were about 6,000

---

[27]Accidents on state or municipal roads are not included in this database.

interstate commerce vehicle infractions and about 7,000 intrastate and private vehicle infractions. Infractions on state or municipal roads are not included in this system.

Mexico Has Participated in Trinational Efforts to Harmonize Land Transportation Standards

Since NAFTA was signed, Mexico has participated in trinational efforts to make U.S., Canadian, and Mexican land transportation standards more compatible. These efforts have included participation in NAFTA's Land Transportation Standards Subcommittee (LTSS). [28] In addition, Mexico has entered into bilateral agreements with the United States on specific commercial motor vehicle safety issues.

According to an LTSS document, the subcommittee has made major accomplishments in the following areas:

- commercial driver's licenses—agreement on a common age (21 years) for operating a vehicle in international commerce;
- language requirements—agreement on a common language requirement (the driver must be able to communicate in the language of the jurisdiction where the commercial vehicle is operating);
- drivers' logbooks and hours-of-service—agreement on safety performance information each country will require from motor carriers; and
- driver medical standards—recognition of several binational agreements as the basis for recognizing driver medical standards.

The LTSS reports that regulatory differences among the countries have made reaching compatibility in some areas difficult. For example, according to a DOT official the three NAFTA countries have not been able to reach agreement on commercial vehicle weight standards, maximum weight limits for truck axles, and dimensions (Mexico's regulations focus on the total length of commercial vehicles while U.S. regulations focus on the length of the trailer).

The United States and Mexico have also entered into binational agreements to ensure the compatibility of commercial vehicle safety standards. Among these are agreements on standards for drug and alcohol tests for drivers and acceptance of commercial driver's licenses issued by

---

[28]The Transportation Consultative Group and the Automotive Standards Council were also created to assist in efforts to harmonize non-standards related measures and automotive manufacturing standards.

the other country. For example, Mexican officials plan to obtain certification for a Mexican federal government laboratory to conduct drug and alcohol tests by 2002. DOT officials said the United States is continuing to work with Mexico on a variety of commercial vehicle safety issues including manufacturing standards and vehicle size and weight limitations.

Mexican Private Sector Reports Making Efforts to Improve Commercial Vehicle Safety

The Mexican private sector reports conducting activities designed to improve the safety of Mexican commercial vehicles. These efforts include conducting inspections to ensure that Mexican vehicles crossing the border meet U.S. safety standards; purchasing new commercial vehicles; and implementing safety rules that, according to Mexican private sector officials, exceed the Mexican government's requirements. Moreover, according to representatives of Mexican private trucking associations, their members have adopted operating standards similar to those of large U.S. trucking companies. Mexican government officials stated that most trucks now used in border drayage operations would not meet their safety standards.

Mexican government officials said that some Mexican trucking companies are purchasing new vehicles in anticipation of operating beyond the commercial zones. According to the Mexican government, the average age of federally registered truck tractors in Mexico is 16 years. In contrast, Mexico's private trucking association, made up of companies that own and operate their own trucking fleets, said that its members' vehicles are relatively new, averaging less than 5 years of age. According to association officials, these newer vehicles are the ones most likely to engage in cross-border trucking beyond the commercial zones.

In Nuevo Laredo, Mexico, a local trucking association established an inspection station to ensure that vehicles belonging to association members meet U.S. standards. According to association officials, this facility is staffed by private maintenance personnel trained by the Texas Department of Public Safety, and inspections are provided free of charge to all member trucking companies. According to a FMCSA state director, this inspection facility, while not able to affix CVSA decals, represents a positive step toward assuring compliance with U.S. and Mexican safety standards.

According to Mexican private industry officials, some Mexican trucking companies have implemented driver education and other operating safety requirements that go beyond the Mexican federal requirements. For example, officials of a Mexican private trucking association said that their members require extensive driver education and use computerized monitoring devices to track driver performance and compliance with company hours of service requirements.

Conclusions

In the 7 years since NAFTA was implemented, the United States and Mexico have taken a number of steps toward achieving closer economic integration. However, despite a strong trading partnership and other ties, cross-border truck safety issues continue to be challenging. Mexico has taken important steps to enhance its regulatory capabilities, including developing key databases containing driver and carrier information and hiring and training inspection personnel. However, Mexico's efforts to increase regulation of its motor carrier industry are relatively new; therefore, it is too early to assess their effectiveness. The U.S. border states and DOT have been increasing the number of safety inspectors inspecting trucks entering the country from Mexico, but it is unclear where additional inspectors will work and how they will share inspection responsibilities. California has built permanent truck safety inspection facilities at two ports of entry and Arizona has work under way to construct another one. At other major crossings, however, only makeshift facilities, at best, are available, and it will be several years until permanent facilities can be built in Texas.

Although some progress has been made, there is continued uncertainty about the extent to which Mexican commercial trucks meet U.S. safety standards. While evidence indicates that limited numbers of Mexican carriers will initially operate beyond the commercial zones, additional work is needed if DOT is to reach its goals of having commercial trucks from Mexico meet U.S. safety standards and achieve similar safety performance results. Further, there is still no coordinated operational plan for how truck safety inspection activities will be conducted or agreements with border states on how best to implement them. There is also no clear agreement on the type and size of facilities that are needed, where they will be located, when they will be finished, or whether state and/or federal inspectors will work there. Such agreements and a coordinated operational plan will become increasingly important to develop and implement as DOT works to address statutory requirements and as cross-border trade grows.

Recommendation for Executive Action

To ensure that Mexican trucks meet U.S. standards, we recommend that the Secretary of Transportation direct the Administrator of the Federal Motor Carrier Safety Administration to develop and implement a coordinated operational truck safety plan at the southwest border. In addition to meeting statutory requirements, this effort should include

- establishing inspection goals;
- taking steps to improve the quality of data to evaluate whether safety goals are being met for both drayage (cross-border shuttle) and long-haul carriers;
- reaching agreements with states and other federal agencies on where inspection facilities will be built, how they will be staffed, and who will operate them; and
- developing a specific timetable for when these actions will be completed.

Agency Comments and Our Evaluation

We received written comments on a draft of this report from the Customs Service, which are reprinted in app. III. We obtained oral comments from DOT, including FMCSA's Associate Administrator for Enforcement and Program Delivery and other officials; the Office of the U.S. Trade Representative, including the Deputy Assistant for Mexico and NAFTA; GSA, including the head of the Border Stations Center; and the Mexican embassy in Washington, D.C. We also provided copies to the Department of State, which did not provide comments, and EPA, which provided two technical comments.

The Office of the U.S. Trade Representative, GSA, and the Customs Service generally agreed with our report's findings and recommendation. DOT officials agreed with our recommendation that they develop a coordinated operational plan to inspect Mexican trucks at the border. However, they strongly emphasized that they were well advanced in their efforts to fulfill our recommendation as well as respond to the new truck safety requirements contained in the fiscal year 2002 DOT appropriations act. DOT officials stated that numerous actions critical to the border's opening are underway or completed and that program implementation timelines and legislative implementation plans are being developed and will be issued shortly. FMCSA officials noted that they are completing detailed planning for hiring and allocating staff; securing new high technology equipment to assist them in accomplishing their mission; and that they have completed a system to track Mexican drivers' U.S. traffic violation history. DOT officials noted that since the passage of DOT's fiscal year 2002 appropriations act, high ranking Department officials will begin meeting immediately with border state officials to coordinate state activities and discuss actions needed to open the border. They noted that detailed work is underway with GSA and Customs to address infrastructure needs at each border port of entry and with the Mexican government to reach agreements on requirements included in the act. DOT officials stated that their past efforts and the efforts they intend to undertake in response to the act provide a comprehensive approach to ensure the safety of Mexican trucks crossing the border. DOT officials also noted that our draft report was completed approximately two weeks before the Congress passed the appropriations act and therefore the information contained in our report predates the requirements specified in the act that the Department must undertake before it can fully open the border.

We have updated the report to reflect the requirements in the fiscal year 2002 DOT appropriations act—requirements that further highlight the importance of our recommendation that DOT develop a coordinated operational plan for truck safety at the Mexican border. We disagree with DOT's comments that they are well advanced in their efforts to implement our recommendation as well as the many requirements contained in the appropriations act. Even prior to the act, DOT had not reached agreements with the states on how to allocate their inspectors or with other federal agencies on the space needed to conduct additional truck inspections. These are basic operational issues that have become more complex with new provisions in the appropriations act, such as the requirement for weigh in motion technologies at the 10 busiest border crossings. In addition, our concerns about DOT's readiness were seconded in comments we received from Customs officials. Customs officials noted that, as of December 2001, they and GSA were still surveying federal facilities along the border to determine where additional space for DOT truck inspections could be found. The additional space becomes more important as a result of the act's provisions for more inspectors, more inspections, and the heightened probability that more space would be needed for Mexican trucks placed out of service. Customs officials expressed continued concern that DOT has not fully developed adequate operational plans to conduct truck safety inspections at federal border facilities.

State and agency officials also provided technical comments to the report. We incorporated these comments, where appropriate, throughout the report.

As agreed with your office, unless you publicly release its contents earlier, we plan no further distribution of this report until 30 days from its issue date. At that time, we will send copies to congressional committees with responsibilities for trade and transportation safety issues; the Secretary of Transportation; the Secretary of State; the U.S. Trade Representative; the Commissioner of the U.S. Customs Service; the Administrator, Environmental Protection Agency; the Administrator, General Services Administration; and the Director, Office of Management and Budget. We will also make copies available to others upon request and on our home page at http://www.gao.gov.

If you or your staff have any questions about this report, please contact me at (202) 512-8979. Key contributors to this report are listed in appendix IV.

Joseph A. Christoff
Director, International Affairs and Trade

Appendix I: Scope and Methodology

To estimate the extent to which Mexican-domiciled commercial trucks are likely to travel beyond the commercial zones, as well as the factors inhibiting or encouraging Mexican carriers to operate beyond these zones, we contacted U.S. federal, state, and local officials, as well as trucking industry representatives, public interest groups, insurance companies and associations, and academics familiar with the Mexican trucking industry. We also reviewed applications filed with the Department of Transportation (DOT) by Mexican commercial motor carriers wishing to operate beyond the commercial zones. In addition, we interviewed Mexican government officials and industry and union representatives, and reviewed statistical data on the Mexican trucking industry.

To obtain information on U.S. government agencies' efforts to ensure that Mexican trucks entering the United States meet safety and emissions standards, we interviewed officials with the Federal Motor Carrier Safety Administration, Federal Highway Administration, Environmental Protection Agency, and the U.S. Trade Representative in Washington, D.C. We also interviewed state and local government officials in the border states and visited ports of entry in Laredo, Texas, Otay Mesa and Calexico, California, and Nogales, Arizona. We reviewed documents provided by DOT, attended congressional hearings on the issue, and reviewed DOT's Notices of Proposed Rulemakings and comments regarding the entry of Mexican trucks into the United States. In addition, we reviewed data contained in DOT's motor carrier management information system to understand its reliability and limitations.

To understand how Mexican government and private sector efforts contribute to ensuring that Mexican commercial vehicles entering the United States meet U.S. safety and emissions standards, we met with officials from the Mexican Embassy in Washington, D.C., as well as the Secretariats of Communication and Transportation, Economy, External Relations, and Environment and Natural Resources in Mexico City. We also reviewed Mexico's regulations dealing with commercial vehicle safety and emissions. However, because of time constraints we were unable to visit the inspection facilities under construction or observe enforcement actions taking place. To understand how the U.S. and Mexican commercial vehicle and driver safety databases function and interconnect, we met with officials from TML, the private contractor working to develop and connect these databases, as well as U.S. and Mexican government officials. We also observed the databases in use in Laredo, Texas; Otay Mesa, California; and Mexico City. To understand the private sector's efforts to improve the safety of their vehicles and their compliance with U.S. safety and emissions standards, we met with Mexican government and private sector officials, toured a large Mexican trucking firm interested in conducting operations beyond the commercial zones, and visited a privately funded inspection facility in Nuevo Laredo, Mexico. To describe efforts to harmonize safety and emissions standards, we attended a conference co-sponsored by the United States and Mexico dealing with vehicle safety and emissions standards, and interviewed DOT and Mexican officials involved in the Land Transportation Standards Subcommittee and other groups.

We conducted our work in accordance with generally accepted government auditing standards from June to November 2001.

Appendix II: Space Available for Truck Inspections at Southwest Border Ports of Entry

The U.S. Customs Service allows state and federal truck inspectors to inspect trucks on its compounds. However, because interagency agreements among FMCSA, GSA, and Customs have not been established, space at such locations is temporary and available only as long as Customs allows its continued use. The exception is in California, where the state operates two permanent truck inspection facilities—Calexico and Otay Mesa–that are located just outside the federal ports of entry. Truck inspection activities do not occur at the federal facilities in California. Table 3 provides an overview of the amount of space currently designated for truck inspection activities at commercial ports of entry along the southwest border.

Table 3: Space Designated for Truck Inspection Activities at Southwest Border Commercial Ports of Entry, as of November 2001

Facility	Number of spaces for state truck inspections	Number of spaces for federal truck inspections	Number of out-of-service spaces for state inspections	Number of out-of-service spaces for federal inspections	Office space for state inspectors (in square feet)	Office space for federal inspectors (in square feet)
Texas						
Veterans International Border Station, Brownsville	2	2	0	10	None	544
Los Indios Border Station, Los Indios	1	2	0	12	None	None
Pharr Border Station, Pharr	2	2	0	8	None	384
Rio Grande City Border Station, Rio Grande City	N/A	3	N/A	3	N/A	None
World Trade Border Station, Laredo	2	12 inspection and out-of-service	0	(see number of spaces)	None	384
Colombia Border Station, Laredo	1	3	0	15	None	384
Eagle Pass II Border Station, Eagle Pass	2	2	0	8 outside of the compound	160	384
Ysleta Border Station, El Paso	3	2	0	8	None	384
Bridge of the Americas Border Station, El Paso	N/A	6	N/A	10	N/A	384
Roma Border Station, Roma	N/A	1	N/A	0	N/A	160
Del Rio Border Station, Del Rio	1	3	0	4	None	None
Presidio Border Station, Presidio	N/A	N/A	N/A	N/A	N/A	N/A

Facility	Number of spaces for state truck inspections	Number of spaces for federal truck inspections	Number of out-of-service spaces for state inspect-ions	Number of out-of-service spaces for federal inspections	Office space for state inspectors (in square feet)	Office space for federal inspectors (in square feet)
Progreso Border Station, Progreso	N/A	1	N/A	0	N/A	160
California						
Tecate Border Station, Tecate	N/A	N/A	N/A	N/A	N/A	N/A
Andrade Border Station, Andrade[a]	N/A	N/A	N/A	N/A	N/A	N/A
Otay Mesa Border Station, Otay Mesa	4 bays	N/A	20	N/A	7,900	N/A
Calexico Border Station, Calexico	4 bays	N/A	20	N/A	7,900	N/A
Arizona						
Naco Border Station, Naco	1	N/A	0	N/A	840	N/A
Sasabe Border Station, Sasabe	1	N/A	0	N/A	460	N/A
Lukeville Border Station, Lukeville	1	N/A	0	N/A	460	N/A
Nogales Border Station, Nogales	1	3	0	0	460	200
Douglas Border Station, Douglas	1	N/A	0	N/A	460	N/A
San Luis Border Station, San Luis	N/A	1	N/A	0	N/A	0
New Mexico						
Columbus Border Station, Columbus	N/A	1	N/A	0	N/A	0
Santa Teresa Border Station, Santa Teresa	N/A	5	N/A	0	N/A	72

N/A – Not applicable. Space has not been designated for truck inspection activities at these ports of entry.

[a]The Andrade Border Station is no longer an official U.S. commercial port of entry.

Source: GSA and California Highway Patrol.

Appendix III: Comments From the U.S. Customs Service

U.S. Customs Service

Memorandum

DATE: December 7, 2001

FILE: AUD-1-OP CN

MEMORANDUM FOR JOSEPH A. CHRISTOFF
DIRECTOR, INTERNATIONAL AFFAIRS
AND TRADE

FROM: Director,
                Office of Planning

SUBJECT: Comments on Draft Audit Report Entitled North
                American Free Trade Agreement: Coordinated
                Safety Inspection System Needed to Ensure
                Mexican Trucks' Compliance with U.S. Standards

Thank you for providing us with a copy of your draft report entitled "North American Free Trade Agreement: Coordinated Safety Inspection System Needed to Ensure Mexican Trucks' Compliance with U.S. Standards" and the opportunity to discuss the issues in this report.

We have reviewed the draft report and have the following comments:

- The report does contain correct statistical information on port traffic.
- Current operational procedures related to federal and state safety inspections are addressed.
- If possible please insert "provided by Customs" after the words temporary space, page 14, middle paragraph, 4th line.
- We agree with the recommendations set forth for executive action on page 31 and would recommend that California/Mexico border be presented as the model process for handling truck safety inspections across the Southwest Border.

We have determined that the information in the audit does not warrant protection under the Freedom of Information Act.

If you have any questions regarding the comments, please have a member of your staff contact Ms. Cecelia Neglia at (202) 927-9369.

TRADITION

★

SERVICE

★

HONOR

William F. Riley

Appendix IV: GAO Contacts and Staff Acknowledgments

GAO Contact

Phillip Herr (202) 512-8509

Acknowledgments

In addition to the person listed above, Jason Bair; Patricia Cazares-Chao; Janey Cohen; Peter Guerrero; Elizabeth McNally; Jose M. Pena, III; Sarah Prehoda; James Ratzenberger; Maria Santos; and Hector Wong made key contributions to this report.

GAO's Mission	The General Accounting Office, the investigative arm of Congress, exists to support Congress in meeting its constitutional responsibilities and to help improve the performance and accountability of the federal government for the American people. GAO examines the use of public funds; evaluates federal programs and policies; and provides analyses, recommendations, and other assistance to help Congress make informed oversight, policy, and funding decisions. GAO's commitment to good government is reflected in its core values of accountability, integrity, and reliability.
Obtaining Copies of GAO Reports and Testimony	The fastest and easiest way to obtain copies of GAO documents is through the Internet. GAO's Web site (www.gao.gov) contains abstracts and full-text files of current reports and testimony and an expanding archive of older products. The Web site features a search engine to help you locate documents using key words and phrases. You can print these documents in their entirety, including charts and other graphics. Each day, GAO issues a list of newly released reports, testimony, and correspondence. GAO posts this list, known as "Today's Reports," on its Web site daily. The list contains links to the full-text document files. To have GAO e-mail this list to you every afternoon, go to www.gao.gov and select "Subscribe to daily e-mail alert for newly released products" under the GAO Reports heading.

Order by Mail or Phone	The first copy of each printed report is free. Additional copies are $2 each. A check or money order should be made out to the Superintendent of Documents. GAO also accepts VISA and Mastercard. Orders for 100 or more copies mailed to a single address are discounted 25 percent. Orders should be sent to:
	
	U.S. General Accounting Office
	P.O. Box 37050
	Washington, D.C. 20013
	
	To order by Phone: Voice: (202) 512-6000
	                            TDD: (202) 512-2537
	                            Fax: (202) 512-6061

Visit GAO's Document Distribution Center	GAO Building Room 1100, 700 4th Street, NW (corner of 4th and G Streets, NW) Washington, D.C. 20013
To Report Fraud, Waste, and Abuse in Federal Programs	Contact: Web site: www.gao.gov/fraudnet/fraudnet.htm, E-mail: fraudnet@gao.gov, or 1-800-424-5454 or (202) 512-7470 (automated answering system).
Public Affairs	Jeff Nelligan, Managing Director, NelliganJ@gao.gov (202) 512-4800 U.S. General Accounting Office, 441 G. Street NW, Room 7149, Washington, D.C. 20548

PRINTED ON RECYCLED PAPER